CALIFORNIA POETRY SERIES

4

Also by Molly Fisk

Salt Water Poems (chapbook, letterpress, 1994)
Terrain (chapbook, with Dan Bellm and Forrest Hamer, 1998)
Surrender (audio tape, 1994)

Molly Fisk

Listening to
Winter

THE ROUNDHOUSE PRESS

Publisher's Cataloging-in-Publication Data
Fisk, Molly.
Listening to winter / Molly Fisk.
p. cm. — (California poetry series ; v. 4)
ISBN: 0-9666691-3-4
1. Incest victims Poetry. I. Title. II. Series
PS3556.I814584L57   1999
811'.54 — dc21   99-41369
                            CIP

Some of the poems in this collection have appeared in the following magazines: *Americas Review, Calyx, Haight Ashbury Literary Journal, Harvard Review, Mānoa, Barnabe Mountain Review, Mudlark* (e-zine), *Onthebus, Passionate Hearts, Poetry East, Poetry Flash, Poetry Now, Point Reyes Light, Survivorship, The Tomcat, ZYZZYVA.*

"Veterans" won first prize in the 1992 National Writers Union Santa Cruz/Monterey Local 7 Competition, appeared in *Love's Shadow* (The Crossing Press, 1993) and *Writing Our Way Out of the Dark* (Queen of Swords Press, 1995); "On The Disinclination to Scream" originally appeared in *Sexual Harassment: Women Speak Out* (The Crossing Press, 1992), and was reprinted in a psychology textbook issued by Athabasca University, Alberta, Canada (1993), and in *Resourceful Woman* (Visible Ink Press, 1993); "Surrender" was included in *The Courage to Heal: A Guide for Survivors of Child Sexual Abuse* (fourth edition, HarperCollins, 1994); "Jupiter" received Honorable Mention in the 1995 Santa Barbara Poetry Festival Contest; "Sugar & Salt" and "The names of streets instead of streets . . ." received Third Prize in the 1995 Villa Montalvo Biennial Poetry Contest. "The Dry Tortugas" won the Billee Murray Denny First Prize in 1996.

This is Volume 4 of the California Poetry Series.
Cover Photo: Mt. Vision, Point Reyes National Seashore. Richard Blair Photography.
Author Photo: Sam Fisk.
Cover and Interior Design: David Bullen Design

The California Poetry Series is published by The Roundhouse Press
and distributed by Heyday Books.

Orders, inquiries, and correspondence should be addressed to:
Heyday Books
P.O. Box 9145
Berkeley, California 94709
phone: 510.549.3564 fax: 510.549.1889
e-mail: roundhouse@heydaybooks.com

Printed in Canada
10   9   8   7   6   5   4   3   2   1

Anthem

Contents

The View from Here

Hunter's Moon

Early December, dusk, and the sky
slips down the rungs of its blue ladder
into indigo. A late-quarter moon hangs
in the air above the ridge like a broken plate
and shines on us all, on the new deputy
almost asleep in his four-by-four,
lulled by the crackling song of the dispatcher,
on the bartender, slowly wiping a glass
and racking it, one eye checking the game.
It shines down on the fox's red and grey life,
as he stills, a shadow beside someone's gate,
listening to winter. Its pale gaze caresses
the lovers, curled together under a quilt,
dreaming alone, and shines on the scattered
ashes of terrible fires, on the owl's black flight,
on the whelks, on the murmuring kelp,
on the whale that washed up six weeks ago
at the base of the dunes, and it shines
on the backhoe that buried her.

Intrigue

I love living in a town so small
it still has a noon whistle.
There is one stop sign,
four-way.
We have our own post office.
People here say hello
and they watch where your car is
at night,
not wanting to miss
a good story.
This makes me want
to park,
flagrantly,
outside the homes
of unsuspecting bachelors,
and lurk in the Parkside
over breakfast,
to hear news
of my own misbehavior.
I am perched
on the edge
of being familiar.

The View From Here

Here, it's the week before Christmas.
Rain heavy all night, some thunder.
The tall bamboo stalks bend their backs,
bowing to the power of water—the pounding
creeks wake us at two, at three,
lifting over their muddy banks, sweeping
fallen branches before them to snag
on the ribbed culverts under the road.
We dress in the pale light of another December
morning, sit drinking our coffee in a bare silence
washed clean of old lovers, failing
parents, the disappointments forgotten,
the stubborn quarrels wrung out of us,
steam from the white cups rising
like breath to wreathe our newborn faces,
halo our tired heads.

Drowning

I.

My body is aching for some kind of minimal dryness
after this coastal damp. Air seeps into me
with the same rhythm this blueblack water moves itself
under beds of kelp—circling, lifting the shaggy fronds and bulbs
in a natural gesture, so human it doesn't resemble the sea.
We are used to froth on the sand, its glint in sunlight
or the flat grey of it under clouds, not this heaving, slowed-down
undulation. But the sound is the same. All over the world,
that slosh against continents.

I'm stalling.
Trying to make all kinds of waiting beautiful.

Under the brown-gold kelp and the seals finning along
like the fish they're after, the loopy somersaults of the otter,
snagged in the black rocks, slick with algae, I have hidden
the hour after my father left my room and before I came downstairs
to set the table for dinner. Its edges are so sharp.
I hoped that decades immersed in the sea would smooth them.
The scene is always the same: a small click as the door shuts,
the silence. My clothes strewn on the floor
and stepped on, or wrinkled and wet underneath me.
The attempt to smooth them.
A damp facecloth between my legs as I look away from the mirror,
brush through my hair. Slowly bringing the old self
back up from wherever it's fallen: elder sister, table-setter.
Standing at the bedroom window looking into the ocean.

II.

Let's return to that silent room,
the back of the father's hand turning as
his fingers curl around the knob, its blue glass
cool in his palm. He twists until the door
opens—another success—its latch clicking
gently behind him. The person
left on the bed, whoever she is,
is still. Sound of her shallow breathing.
Her clothes not torn. Her flesh unbruised.
She rolls onto her side and stares at the line
of familiar books without seeing their titles.
Now she is ours, we can make her do anything.
Let's have her stand and walk to the sink to wash—
a sweet-smelling girl is always nicer.
She never cries. Prop her beside the window
and let her look out at the spinning world, let her ear
be tuned to the unsmothered cries of the living:
starlings, beetles, the desperate fish.
She'll never be lonely.

Jupiter

I wake up at four with the bright white beads of a headache
strung behind my eyes, shifting and clicking, an abacus

counting out sorrows. Click. I am alone. Click. I haven't had
children yet. Will anyone know me or love me?

Regret. All morning I count change into the outstretched
hands of strangers as if I were spilling the letters of my name

into their open palms. Expecting a flicker of recognition.
I bag their maps and books—give half a smile, directions.

I wonder when my life will turn out. Where's the assurance
we had as kids, when things made sense and dinnertime

always came at dusk, a call from the porch, the pale globes
of whiffle balls glowing like moons at the lawn's shadowy edge.

                                        Outside the windows
it's black, and cool for August. Sagittarius chases the scorpion

slowly across the southern sky. In Latin the word for planet
is wanderer: Jupiter pulls at the end of his orbit, invisibly

leashed to the sun, but from here it looks like he's weaving,
drunk, among the mythical pictures—Hunter, Bears, Dog,

Virgin—drawn by people already centuries dead.
Night after night I watch him roam, and in every American town

there are others, lying flat-backed in wheat fields and ball parks,
empty lots, or leaning against a window like this, with a glass

still half-full of water, aspirin swallowed,
foreheads pressed to the dark.

The Language

As a child in California I did not learn Spanish
like everyone else, the practical language.
In college I studied Norwegian, carefully placing
the *l*s out on the end of my tongue,
letting my hesitant breath swirl around them.

> *l* as in *melk* (milk), *flink* (clever)
> *l* as in *velkommen til Norge*

Whenever I could, I turned north—
toward the cool blue eyes and red beards,
the wooden ships and churches, reindeer,
cloudberries, snow.

> *reinsdyr, møltebaer, snø.*

What is the longing for all light? For none?
Like every heroine, I wanted to understand my life.

Whether or not you believe in coincidence
and whether or not you like it, the word *sex*
in Norwegian still means six.

And if everything is a sexual metaphor—
if the Vikings populated two continents
by raping the native women, and if my father,
whom I still love, sailed to Norway
and brought me back a patterned sweater
before I was even born, if he was the one
who wandered into the wrong rooms at night,
where the inhabitants could not protest
because they didn't speak the language,
then why would I try to learn Spanish?

Midnight

I was the girl who grew up
and went as far from home
as she could travel, to the country
her father loved the most, walked
down its narrow roads, leaned back into
the cracked leather seats of its hurrying
trains.

        The girl who watched
mountains tick by in all-night twilight,
framed in the windows like photographs,
her fingers laced in her quiet lap, coat folded
under a tired cheek against the blinking glass.
See how she carries it like a blessing:
the weariness of those who can't go back,
who go on trying to balance rebellion
and obedience. Like the good child in a fairy tale
she found what she was sent for: loneliness
and humor—her vast inheritance.

        She found color and it moved her.
Black peaks with their ragged shoulders pressed
into an orange sky. Two women on the platform:
a red scarf binds the tall one's hair—both heads
suddenly thrown back in laughter. The shaded green
of northern summer, and in winter: snow as blue
and white as snow. A flock of yellow-shuttered houses
on a hillside—squat, impassive. Perched like seagulls
waiting out a storm. And the light—endless light,
the kind of light you long for, path to Heaven,
all your days torn from their edges—
the flowers bowing beside the tracks
open their faces to it at midnight.

On The Disinclination To Scream

If I had been a ten year old stranger
and you had tripped me in a dark alley, say,
downtown, instead of our mutual living room,
I'm sure I would have screamed.

If, in the alley, you had straddled me as fast—
your knees clamping my elbows into asphalt,
not the blue Chinese dragons
of our living room rug,
I might have been quiet there, too.

When you opened my mouth
with your heavy flat thumbs,
filled it with pain and flesh—
I would have choked in the alley,
as anyone would choke.

But if you had groaned then, and stood up,
walked away from the dark street
leaving me to vomit and shake alone,
I might have been saved.

I could describe you to policemen.
Perhaps their composite would match your photo
in the Harvard Reunion guide.
Your fingerprints, lifted from the collar of my dress,
might be found in Coast Guard files.

If they never found you and there was no trial
I could have gone home to people who loved me:
horrified, enraged, they would plot revenge
and rock me to sleep in soft arms.

I would have been frightened, maybe forever,
of alleys, strange men, and the dark—
but encouraged by the world, who would hate you on my behalf.
I would have been as safe as a ten year old can be.

Instead, I rose quietly from the Chinese rug
and went upstairs to wash.
No sound escaped me.
I couldn't afford to throw up,
and it wasn't the first time.

Explanation

Finally I just gave up and became an animal.
I slept when I was tired,
sometimes dropping in mid-stride,
curling into a knot on the sunny floor.
I ate raw food at odd hours,
wiped my mouth on the back of my hand,
stopped brushing my hair.
The phone rang, but I didn't answer it.
Mail lay unopened on the stairs. Flowers
drooped in dry pots. Dust sifted down
from the ceiling in hazy swirls.
I left the windows open.
After a few weeks I grew
accustomed to it, sank deeper
into my actual body, learned to love
the hours as they passed.
I let go of the spinning
human world and walked in the hills at night
under a changing moon.
Deer swung their heads toward me.
I sat beside them in their beds of creaking grass
listening to crickets ticking in the heat.
I cooled my skin in the ocean, licked
the crusted salt from my arms.
In time, my throat forgot to speak,
it lost the bright angles of consonants,
the dark sloping vowels. It joined the chorus
of mute life with a kind of hum.

Where is the Lake of Dreams?

The names of streets instead of streets . . .

Dan Bellm

When, in Oslo, I skied down the main street, pushing off
against the white rim of the world, gliding past
the train station and the famous nude statues, I spoke
a language of my own, the *gammelnorsk* Margit taught me
from before the war mixed with a little *grisprat*
I learned in Vågå. I got along, but there is something
about living in a language you don't own that teaches you
the first steps of dying. Without the slanted American puns
and dumb jokes, nothing special, just what anyone
would know, I was diminished, I was not myself,
and I carry it, mixed in with cold nights and lilting vowels:
chilled breath from the other side of heaven.

I will always belong to the Spanish names of California,
but I liked the pushed-forwardness of that arctic speech,
the precarious ring of those *l*s against the top of my teeth,
suspended like icicles: *Jeg elsker deg, du elsker meg,*
velkommen til Norge, and the way you have to almost smile
to get the *e* right, hardly opening your mouth, since at that latitude
everything, even the language, is based on trying to stay warm.
I was someone in Norwegian but I don't know who —
and when a Viking wrapped me in his sweatered arms
against the wind and called my name into the northern sky,
I couldn't help it — under my breath I said *San Francisco,*
I said *Divisadero,* I said *Anza, Balboa, Cabrillo.*

Neighbor

Some afternoon I may back him up
against the cool wall of his own
garage, lower his door with my left
hand, hold his shirt with my right,
the knobbed collarbone smooth underneath
my fingers, my thumb pressed against
flat breast muscle. He won't protest
or move, he'll be delirious about it,
I've been catching his eye for months
when we pass on the street, stop to talk
about nothing and the weather and roses.
I try to avoid situations like this,
even though I like his eyes, because
he lives with a woman of his own—I don't
like to interrupt people. But on a hot
afternoon I may want his arms around me;
I like the sound of cloth stripped fast
off skin and the expectant shiver
when you start to do something
a man wants you to do to him.

Surface Tension

It's like the instant your canoe tilts
over the edge, the way it hangs
for a beat or two, reluctant to leave
calm water, then shoots forward
to meet the rapid; the second
after they've fired the rocket into the air
on the 4th of July and it hasn't opened yet,
it's just one dot of light, you hold
the silvery shower of stars behind your eyes,
remembering last year, childhood,
just for a second, until it blooms;
like the moment when, tangled
in a half-lit room, he comes
and you're watching him, the hard breath,
his back arched against your palms,
the way he cannot stop his legs from shaking.

The Answer to a Sportscaster's Prayer

My vagina is the best waitress in an all-night diner
Off 1-49, slapping nickels and quarters on the counter
With one hand, pouring coffee with the other,
Calling *meatloaf-double sunnyside-whole wheat*
Over her shoulder and winking at the trucker
Half-way through a midnight ride out of Denver
Who came in here just to see that smile, and my vagina

Is a software tycoon leaning back in a swivel chair
At ten in the morning—no one can buy that kind
Of confidence—the profit margin swelling,
Five new ideas in the planning stage, R&D and marketing
Working together for once and the roll-out on schedule,
Beta-testing commenced, she's looking forward
To an end run past the competition, and my vagina is the answer

To a sportscaster's prayer, grey two-year old, nervous as usual,
Head down through the gate and then she suddenly
Settles into a faster pace than even her jockey
Expected, on the instant replay you can see the startled look
Cross his face before he leans on her neck and shouts *come on*
Girl, you can do it, get us the hell out of here, come on
Baby, baby, baby, BABY, bring us all the way home.

Ford F150

Do you remember
parking your red truck
at that rest stop in Minnesota
at ten in the morning the day before
Christmas, fifteen below and a light
snow falling, so glad to be out of
your mother's house we tore into
each other as soon as we could,
the cab steaming up, it must have been
obvious what we were doing
but no one drove by, my hands under
your hands, our mittened fingers
splayed on the dash, elbows locked, hips
rocking the chassis, the top of my head
just grazing the windshield, your breath
warming the back of my neck, one
shoulder wedged up to the passenger
window, one boot braced on
the gearshift's base, our knees fitted together
like stackable chairs, the impossible angle:
you kept slipping out, the shivery friction
of denim on denim, unzippered oasis
where flesh met flesh, the creak of
the seat when we couldn't stop moving,
a song on the radio I can't remember but
when it was over we hummed it all the way home.

Red River

It's true, I could hold you
after a night of laughing, say,
watching Montgomery Clift
and John Wayne trail their cattle
through Mexico, southern Texas.
And when the movie's over
and the rinsed dishes are shining
in the drainer like faces of good children,
the wine bottle set by the back door,
glowing faintly green in the dark,
nighthawks will scatter their sharp cries
into the streetlamp's yellow halo
and the moon will begin her steady
descent, and you'll find your way somehow
inside me, tonguing my breasts, gently
closing my eyelids with the callused tips
of your fingers, bending me
backward over the sofa's ready arm,
but it's not enough, I want you
closer. I want you to pull me inside you,
open your warm skin like a raccoon coat
and wrap it around me, I want to inhabit
the tightening muscles, curl up in your dense,
well-marrowed bones, feel what you touch,
roll the gold vowels of my own name
around in your mouth before they're spoken,
our blood drifting down through the same
dark river, mingled together. I don't know
which is worse: coming, or watching you come.

Walking Down Franklin Street

It's still there, the weary three-decker.
It still leans inward from the outside walls.
I used to wake up in that house
and lie in bed alone, smiling, looking out
the tall windows at early cars
going by, a neighbor walking his old
slow dog before work. He'd move
out of sight, leave me with sunlight
that spilled in and made a warm
lake of the floor.

Nothing is as simple as it looks.
The man I loved and lived with once threw me
against that front hall wall—stars
floated lightly on the surface
of my eyes, little pieces of white plaster dust
drifted in the air around us. Time went so slow.
I had a chance to think about the precarious
lives of women: anonymous dark Egyptians
hauling water; pioneers in checked sunbonnets
who trudged beside their wagons;
nuns bent over herb gardens in fourteenth century France.
Waiting for his next move, I saw all the women who were held
against walls, I could hear their thoughts. We were
the same person. Our breasts lifted and fell
in time to each others' ragged breathing, our eyes
slid briefly toward the door before
dragging themselves to his face—the human face
irate: corded neck, eyes raging black, the mouth
contorted into that painful,
unsustainable shape. No one
could hold on to it.

Where is the Lake of Dreams?

In the belled, hollow hours before dawn
I stand in the dark and watch you sleep. Alone
on the wide bed of the night you are peaceful,
one hand curled under your cheek, an arm
flung out. The distance between us is narrowest here
in silence, I can be near you, just out of reach
with my back pressed flat against the cool
glass of the window. My eyes follow the trail
my tongue has traced along the square edge of your hip,
trestle of ribs lifting and falling, the innocent fold
where shoulder and armpit meet. The long-dead
light of Arcturus drifts across your palm,
illuminating love-line, life-line, callused fingers.
If I could speak, and you could hear me, I would say
this is love—one body framed in a window, guarding the other.

Beauty

Sugar & Salt

Afterwards, you're never the same—
you leave larger tips than you can really
afford, remembering the tired feet,
pantyhose stripped down over knees
and calves so sore that massaging them,
collapsed on the edge of your unmade bed,
didn't help. Living from week to week
on crumpled dollars stuffed in a bureau drawer.
Greasy film on your hair and skin. Clothes
stained with coffee. You instinctively wipe
the tables at McDonald's before you get up to go.
In busy cafes you stack the finished dishes
to one side, return the busboy's harried smile.
Admire some smooth choreography
behind the counter. You never spill salt
or aimlessly tear at colored packets
of sugar, waiting for this or that lover
to find his way back from the bathroom of a diner.
Your face shines with a recognizable patience.
The flung fork picked up from the floor, stray
spoons retrieved from between the seats:
it's automatic, a habit you barely realize—
the first to get up, reaching for napkins,
pulling the heated bread out of the oven.
You wipe the drop of soup from the bowl's lip
before setting it down in front of your son
or your mother. And in those crowded rooms—
Thanksgiving or a family wedding—the soft call
of your elbow's crease, confident, aching
again for the balanced plate.

Beauty
for Vierra & Friends

You will almost see it, beyond the purple and silver
hairclips parked on the counter completely ready,
like a fleet of idling steamshovels. And next to them,
in plastic bowls of opalescent color waiting
to be brushed over gray, over brown, the familiar strands
lifted and snipped, spritzed with mysterious solutions
and scented foam. It's nestled between the smiling
regiment of bottles, just over there, where the turquoise
Logics Remoisturizing Shampoo meets Sebastian's
Performance *Active* Texturizer, glowing quietly ochre
behind white cursive letters. The window-glass, tight
in its teal-blue frame, reflects it, like light off the edge
of the first morning you were born, and it brightens
the black adjustable swivel chairs, patient
beside each molded sink—it softens the cold chrome
faucets, the chipped linoleum tiles. Sitting in the yellow
naugahyde seat of a Fifties hood dryer, you'll think
it's winking back at you from all six mirrors, and just like love
there is nothing missing and no one is spared,
as the whir from somebody's hand-held blow dryer
shuffles the glossy pages of *Vogue,* Beauty will enter
your perfect spine, and this time you will let her all the way in,
you will sit still without saying anything.

The Goodbye

A little edgy, we peer into the crystal ball
of street maps, the new town smoothed
across her kitchen table, hoping wood smoke,
in fine plumes, or the smell of rain on asphalt
will rise from tangled blue and yellow lines
to comfort us with the familiar.
We want to see ourselves next year
walking with her there, or anywhere.

She finds new men to wrap her last
weeks around. Calls us, breathless,
with stories of dancing slow, their funny remarks
in bed, and doesn't know if she'll be ready
for the movers in time, there's so much to do,
cedar or mothballs? What about
all the unsorted files?

We listen and nod. Recommend mothballs
because they're stronger, and smile
the cracked smiles of all who stay behind—
our good faces obeying the rules
while rebellious hearts thrash in our chests.

In her house the aisles between
brown cardboard boxes narrow,
the walls become more bare—absent
photos leave a trail of unexpected
windows where the paint still glows new.
We help her pack but tiptoe around the fact
that she's going, lean farther into the future,

as if it could hold us up—the improbable
miracle of a job she didn't look for, apartment
rented over the phone. The weeks collapse

into days and then hours, persimmons
ripen on the tree in her yard. The last
odds and ends—playing cards, a facecloth—
are dropped into the last box and sealed in.

The men are temporary, indistinguishable.
We look at them the way one might glance
at faces in a crowd, waiting for the first baton to spin
its crazy circles in the air above a homecoming parade,
the bass drums beating out of sight while we tip forward
on the balls of our feet to catch a glimpse of the band.

A band perhaps like this one, at the high school
down the hill, practicing its marches in August's fading light
as she drives away, honking her horn and waving to us,
the sweet and sour notes floating together,
invisible in the silvered sky above her empty house.

Love Poem
for John Mendel

Shit, how the body betrays us. Chronic ache in the back
turning cancerous overnight, at the end of a century

we hoped to live through—how bitterness makes us suddenly
hate the sun, the palm tree's blue shadow flickering

in a thoughtless breeze, the oblivious, rolling ocean.
Life doesn't love us back—like a beautiful woman

we wanted too much, it walks on surely without us.
But the disappointment isn't permanent—it's too tiring,

for one thing, and the truth is humans were born to love
this world, we can't help it. We take the living flesh of another

into our arms, whisper into the pink shell of an ear,
our lips brushing the bent wrist, the collarbone's wing.

Or the mouthpiece of a telephone—hollow bones
in our ears ringing with a friend's voice: perfect noise.

We drink what liquids they'll allow us after the radiation
and taste the familiar made new, our throats opening

with mortal joy, like the throats of egrets open
to the shining fish. We are alive. It is everything.

Another Letter to Peggy

Yes, everyone thinks it would bother me,
not just because it's a single room
but because it's the one where
my father lived. I have no explanation.
The week after he died we came out here,
four tall kids and Mom, walked around touching
the furniture, the photographs of ourselves,
telling stories about him we already knew.
We drew straws for his things and I kept winning.
The others were furious but I hardly noticed,
I was so bereaved, like them.
We floated somewhere above the ground,
closer to death ourselves, light with grief.
He had us so much in his thrall
it was like lifting out the sun
and watching planets unable to orbit, spinning
in random concert, their various masses
leaning into each other and swinging away.
This was when Mom made her famous
remark— *You wouldn't be this upset*
if it were me who died, she said,
and put her head down on the kitchen counter.
It was the first time I felt mortal. He was gone,
I knew she couldn't look outside herself
to help us, and I was grown, alone,
the oldest, first on the list, the sky
cracked open and black stairs already descending.
Roofs flew off the tops of houses I stayed in,
I couldn't sleep.
Did I ever tell you we ate
some of his ashes?
We swallowed the little chips of bone
with his own leftover orange juice.
They tasted like nothing, chalky pills.

And he didn't come back.
It's a circle now,
the way I slept next to the ashes
in their plastic box before
we scattered them — so when,
later, I remembered his weight on me
it wasn't completely surprising. I knew
there had to be some heavy price
to inspire that kind of love,
some kind of balance.

A Question About the World

All this rain
has flooded the field mice
out of their burrows. Death
sits on fence posts, watching
with its bead-black eyes.
Today it doesn't need height—
the telephone poles, their singing
wires—to mask the old intention.
The mice run for the shelter of hedges
and ditches, their slicked-back fur
shining against new green land.

They are so smooth, the hawks,
lifting their silent
feathered arms, gliding an inch
from the tips of the grass.
A casual swipe, almost
a caress, and the soft brown bite
is airborne, speared.
It looks easy.

Whose side are you on?
The purposeful bird, beautiful
and hungry? Or the busy,
oblivious mouse?

Extend your gaze a few miles
down this road. There's a blue car
parked behind the playground.
Someone waits inside it,
watching children—his hands
rest lightly on the wheel, his eyes
never waver.

Is this the same? I'm asking you.
Is this also part of the natural world?

Moment

And now I am expected to love myself, to love both small hands
that gripped the balusters until their knuckles whitened, the blue

eyes looking down over a gleaming curve of railing into the hall below,
I am supposed to dismantle the face of that girl, stroke her cheek

until the jaw unclenches, speak gently enough to bring tears up
from their locked room and into her eyes—I can't do it.

Her father is behind her, the crease in his dark blue suit pants
brushing against the backs of her thighs, her velvet skirt

bunched at the waist, white Carter Spanky Pants, size 6x, pooled
over the patent leather shoes on her feet, I am supposed to *love* this?

the moan rising up from his tight throat, a sound like rocks
hurled over a cliff, breaking on the valley floor two hundred feet below,

I am looking down at the star my mother made, pinned to the top
of our Christmas tree, I am not going crazy, my brothers and sisters

are already out in the car, I swore I would never be caught on the stairs
again and I was caught, it is this bright failure I love, clear inheritance,

the only true thing that is mine.

Surrender

When the truth came to me,
slipped into my house in its white
robes, its face open as my face,
its heart obvious and trusting,
I stood calmly in the front hall
and did not move to bar the door.

When the truth laid its cool hand
on my sleeve and said,
Come with me, it's time, I went
quietly. She led me into the past,
through the backyards I once
knew, bedrooms and kitchens;
we sat in my father's car and talked.

I was shivering in my thin skin
and crying readily by this time: terrified,
furious. She offered her own consolation—
no false pats on the hand and no shoulder
to lean on, I had to learn to stand upright
or bend on my own. In her clear voice
the truth offered all she has to give us:
Herself, and the stern comfort
of belonging to this world.

Anthem

Couples

Hold on to what you remember,
this exact summer, everything unchanged,
the blue Ford Falcon with its handle-crank
back window rolled down driving
the green length of Argilla Road,
all the cousins under ten then,
eight of us crammed into the way-back
singing "Day Tripper," singing "Can't Buy Me Love."
We are salted and sandy, shreds of brown kelp
still caught in our bathing suits,
the melting ice cream cones already
thrown out the window; we are baked;
we are quarreling and happy.

The desultory remarks of four tired parents
float over our heads and into that summer:
they are thinking of gin, and tonic,
and four o'clock volleyball, getting the kids
washed, shucking the corn and feeding them,
do we have enough hot dog buns, stopping
at Aggie's for another pack of cigarettes.
The muscular fathers, up in the front seat,
are trading old jokes and both looking forward
to the low-backed sleeveless cotton dresses
of the other men's wives and our mothers know it,
but nothing is wrong yet, everyone's cheerful.

Nauset

When my grandmother said *Act like a post*
I slid down to my knees and held completely still.
We watched the gull chicks gradually relax
and lift out of their camouflage in footprints
and tire tracks. As soon as they ran she'd be up
to throw her shadow over them, tripping a little
in the loose sand, and where they froze again
at the predator I fixed my eyes so I could direct her.
Rafts of ducks floated on the swell outside the breakers,
Least terns screamed overhead and the whole
colony of gulls dive-bombed us. She carried
the scar of one's bill along the length
of her part, which was why we wore hats.
I carry the high shriek of gulls into sleep
years later, sand still in everything, the blue glare
squinting my eyes while her voice says
Hold him gently and she slips the silver band
around a yellow leg, her gnarled, meticulous hand
working the pliers to twist it shut and the heat
still rising and the surf banging.

Veterans

for Dorianne

Our fathers padded down separate halls
in different years, to find us. She shifts
in her chair when I say I couldn't help it:
that's what bodies are made for. I didn't
want to, but I came. I was four, then eight,
twelve—I didn't know how to stop him.

We are reminiscing in her backyard
like army buddies from boot camp shipped
to different fronts of the same long war.
We didn't come home in trash bags—

we are here, under the fruit trees, nominally
whole—no wheel chairs, no bourbon bottles
under the bed; we carry scars invisible
to the untrained eye.

Our eyes are honed like lasers, they're the eyes
of hunted animals gleaming in the dark,
ciphering through choked air
across a kitchen table, measuring
the danger in every quiet sound.

For her it wasn't arousing, she waited
for him to be done. Once, her body took off
on its own, responding—she wrestled herself
to a standstill, right at the edge of the world.

I got addicted to the feeling, made myself
come every day of my childhood. She says
her boyfriend taught her, at eighteen,
on the phone. We laugh at that—
with a pillow? On the phone?

Her dog barks. We come back
to what we live with now. I've given up—
at thirty-six I sleep alone, ignore
the breasts he fondled, the hips
I had to watch him lift in his broad hands.
My body shudders close to men,
holding down the scream.

She has gone the other way. Her coming
is a kind of armor—she's piling up sensation
the way I gather distance, still trying to build
a rampart against those indelible nights
we carry in our shuttered hearts like glass.

This is the Story of My Life

In the middle of the day, in Chicago, I sneak away from my desk and go to see the movie my father died watching. I ask Jon if he'll go with me, but he knows better.

After we come home from swimming I walk the 10 blocks to my best friend's house with wet hair and horrify her mother on both counts.

I decide to seduce Jamison at Julie's wedding and the grass stains eventually do come out of my borrowed dress. Twenty years later, Sari sends me the dress instead of giving it to the Salvation Army.

On my twenty-fourth birthday I try cocaine for the first time and talk for approximately six hours.

In between babysitting jobs Peggy teaches me to stack onion rings from Jack in the Box on her mother's blue mustang's antenna, and then drive fast enough down 101 so they fly off.

Sally and I drive from Orleans to Cambridge and are so high we don't notice a thirty degree increase in temperature until we pass a sign that says 78 degrees, which at first we think is broken until we notice that everyone on the street is wearing tank tops and shorts. I turn off the heat and open the windows, and Sally takes off her wool coat, turtleneck, and silk long john top and rides the rest of the way home in only her black bra and sunglasses.

We go every day of the summer to Paul Daly's Swim School, where I learn to back-stroke, jackknife, and tread water. The vending machine sells nothing but creamsicles.

The first Jay throws me against the front hall wall and that becomes the snapshot of our relationship, even though I still love the way he kidnaps me from work during snowstorms and drives us to Crane's Beach with champagne on ice in a spackle bucket.

While memorizing French verbs for the College Boards I place the engraved
silver teaspoons and linen napkins my grandmothers have given me into
a suitcase and don't tell anyone it's my hope chest.

When I meet the man I'm going to marry, I think: "this is just an experiment
until I find the right one." I still kind of think this.

My father has his fourth heart attack in a movie theater in San Francisco, as the
final credits are rolling, and someone actually gets to say "Is there a doctor
in the house?" and there are five, but none of them can save him.

I finally stop doing cocaine because it drives me to eat aspirin and drink beer
before breakfast, just to calm down, and I've never even liked beer. I turn
to Ecstasy instead.

Much later I win first prize in a poetry contest for a poem about incest, using my
real name.

The third Jay and I break my bed at three in the morning, but luckily I have a
first floor apartment so no one calls the police.

My mother and my aunt both get divorced the same spring and my uncle says to
my father, his favorite and only ex-brother-in-law, "We are now connected
by something so tenuous nothing can break it."

When I hear my father has died, I get into my new dress anyway and go to four
Christmas parties because I don't think I can stand to be alone. I ring Fred
and Margot's doorbell at six the next morning and they pull me, fully-
clothed, into bed between them.

Longing

Please, let me go back.
Let me close this half-read book,
stand up, and walk backward
away from the setting sun,
the tall windows opening on the Pacific,
over the threshold of this house
I have lived in. I'll pack the car, drive
backward across the tawny hills,
washed by the scent of bay and oak,
blue shadows spilling down their crevasses,
into a different autumn.

I'll wake up in those motels
again, retrace my steps through glowing
dusk toward lit truck stops.
The eggs will reappear, yolks
gold on thick white plates.
The spilled coffee will lift
back into too-full cups, the waitresses
swallow their blunt apologies.
Early, unexpected snow will rise
into Wyoming air along the interstate.
Dry leaves will gather themselves,
circle the trunks of poplar and cottonwood
lining the Platte—red and yellow
drift up to rustle, supple again,
on each bare branch.
I promise, I'll be content.

Let me go back. I'll refold the maps and
mail them back to Triple A.
The odometer's little numbers will spin
the other way. Let me go home to the frame house
on Story Street with its mansard roof

and painted railings. Let me trip
on the brick sidewalks of Cambridge again.
I'll be Denis' girl, or Jay's, I'll never wonder
if something's missing. I want their fingers
tracing soft lines up my thighs, the warm
mouths hunting mine, trembling bodies lowered
over me on lost afternoons. Let me give up
understanding and belong to my family again.
Give me the simple quarrels with my mother,
my sister's late night phone calls. I want
my laughing brothers and Thanksgiving dinner
with all our cousins. Let me take the long
road: down the turnpike into Boston
on that same September morning,
back to ignorance.

Apart

Why are their clothes on while you sit
naked on the kitchen table?
Your hair hasn't reddened yet, it's blonde
—you're under ten. You sort of have breasts
but not really. They are covered
with hands now; their hands
are everywhere; your body is listening.
It begins to answer, waits, then,
lulled into the growing warmth,
forgetting the very peculiar scene,
you come, and Grandpa says, *I told you*
the Devil was in her. He slaps you hard
across the mouth. *We have to get him out.*

You begin to come apart. A part of you
rises to stand at the window—
you measure the length of a day lily stem
pressed against the glass, bent
with the blank weight
of its own green leaves. They lift you
from the table, carry you outdoors.
It doesn't really matter what happens.
The lily is the color of your favorite
doll's calico dress. In slow motion
your aunt ties your hands
to the broken frame of a screen door.
She has pale grey paint on her thumb.
Your mother opens the two-pound
can of honey. Your father spoons
it onto your stomach, spreads it
like hand lotion inside your thighs,
on the soles of your feet.
He pours it over your face and into your hair.

There is a blue-legged spider swinging
from a drainpipe—it rests a minute
on the lily's back, and then continues
down. The part of you standing by the window
surveys the scene on the lawn.
The birch leaves are singing
their mid-August song. Grandpa rolls up
the sleeves of his old plaid shirt
and reaches into the hive.
It turns out bees aren't quiet
while eating, they make a noise
like tiny chain saws; they stumble around;
they sting. Under closed lids
you can feel them whirring, caught
in your eyelashes—you can't scream:
if you open your mouth
the ones on your lips will crawl in.
And besides, who will help you?

Anthem

Always the heart repeats its true name.
The twin bellows of lung fill and soften, and soften
further, and fill, a song heard in the pines,
in the eaves of houses emptied in summer—
a gurgle of laughter, water. I am alone,
like the fox, alert on an unused road, still.
Listening. Wild radish and lupine, larkspur,
the grasses: bright flags of the generous world.
And since *yes* requires its answering *no,*
the snapped neck of a deer splayed half-across the path
and a pair of raucous crows. Farther along, something,
a vole or hapless mouse, gathered and dispersed
in the delicate cough ball of an owl.
This is when it gets difficult: learning how to live.
A sliver of burnished ocean sings beyond the hills
and the sturdy heart blesses its own reflection.

The Dry Tortugas

They were building a house in the Dry Tortugas,
less for the solitude there than the open eyes
of a swallowtailed hummingbird they had seen once
on a fishing trip—the early Fifties, he reeling in
an oversized yellowfin, Humphrey Bogart
facing the wind, one foot on the rail in *To Have and Have Not,*
she whistling the stuttered call of the Amazonian kingfisher,
and singing in Spanish to flocks of Bonaparte gulls.
It comes to nothing in the end, though the land
is paced off and measured and two palms felled
to expand the view, a road graded the requisite mile,
and some of their friends fly down from New York
to surprise them, circle the islands all morning, gleeful and chic
in their 4-seater Cessna (he's something exalted at Chase),
and later the bottles of Myer's and Appleton Gold sweat
dark rings on the terrace flagstones, and someone's pink
lipstick makes delicate kissprints along the rim of her glass.
No one has told me what happened—his heart attack
in Guatemala, her premonition about the wide
and empty view—or the world swinging in
with its usual brazen distractions—but they framed
the architect's plans of the house, and this
is what I inherit, a rendering in colored pencil:
what they were dreaming before I was born.

1. "Hunter's Moon" is dedicated to the towns of Stinson Beach, Bolinas, Olema, Inverness, and Point Reyes Station, California and was written at the time of the Inverness Ridge fire of 1995.
2. "The View from Here" is for Sandy and Martin; its title comes from a poem of the same name by Martin Koeppel.
3. The title of "The names of streets instead of streets . . ." is a phrase from Dan Bellm's poem "Delle Avenue" in *Buried Treasure,* Cleveland State University Press, 1999.
4. The Lake of Dreams, *Lacus Somniorum,* is on the near side of Earth's only moon.
5. The epigraph for "Anthem" comes from Mary Oliver's poem "Rain," from *New and Selected Poems* by Mary Oliver, Beacon Press, 1992.

VOLUME 1: *One Hand on the Wheel* by Dan Bellm
VOLUME 2: *In Danger* by Suzanne Lummis
VOLUME 3: *The Dumbbell Nebula* by Steve Kowit
VOLUME 4: *Listening to Winter* by Molly Fisk
VOLUME 5: *Wishbone* by Priscilla Lee

The *California Poetry Series* celebrates the great diversity of aesthetics, culture, geography, and ethnicity of the state by publishing work by poets with strong ties to California. Books within this series are published quarterly and feature the work of a single poet, or in some cases two or more poets with a clear affinity. Malcolm Margolin of Heyday Books is publisher; Joyce Jenkins of Poetry Flash is editor.

An advisory board of prominent poets and cultural leaders has been assembled to encourage and support California poetry through this book series. These include Alfred Arteaga, Chana Bloch, Christopher Buckley, Marilyn Chin, Karen Clark, Wanda Coleman, Gillian Conoley, Peter Coyote, Jim Dodge, Lawrence Ferlinghetti, Jack Foley, Jewelle Gomez, Robert Hass, Jane Hirshfield, Fanny Howe, Lawson Inada, Jaime Jacinto, Diem Jones, Stephen Kessler, William Kistler, Carolyn Kizer, Steve Kowit, Dorianne Laux, Philip Levine, Genny Lim, Suzanne Lummis, Lewis MacAdams, David Mas Masumoto, David Meltzer, Deena Metzger, Carol Muske-Dukes, Jim Paul, Kay Ryan, Richard Silberg, Gary Snyder, Dr. Kevin Starr, David St. John, Sedge Thomson, Alan Williamson, and Gary Young.

California Poetry Series books are available at bookstores nationwide or by subscription ($40.00/year). For more information:
Heyday Books
P.O. Box 9145
Berkeley, California 94709
phone: 510.549.3564   fax: 510.549.1889
e-mail: roundhouse@heydaybooks.com

CALIFORNIA POETRY SERIES